You're a daughter of the King

You're a daughter of the King

CONDUCT YOURSELF AS SUCH

IVONNAH ERSKINE

You're a Daughter of the King
Conduct yourself as such.

Copyright © 2018

Scriptures marked NLT are taken from the HOLY BIBLE, NEW LIVING TRANSLATION (NLT): Scriptures taken from the HOLY BIBLE, NEW LIVING TRANSLATION, Copyright© 1996, 2004, 2007 by Tyndale House Foundation. Used by permission of Tyndale House Publishers, Inc., Carol Stream, Illinois 60188. All rights reserved. Used by permission.

All rights reserved. This text or any section thereof may not be reproduced, scanned, transmitted, recorded, uploaded for electronic methods or used in any manner whatsoever without the expressed written consent of the author except for the use of a book review.

ISBN: 978-1-7325952-2-4

eBook ISBN: 978-1-7325952-4-8

Library of Congress Control Number: 2019901688

Table of Contents

Thank You: I Love You..........................6

Foreword: My Inspiration........................7

Section One: Don't Believe the Hype.......9

Self Reflection

Section Two: Keep it Tight............49

Self Reflection

Section Three: R.E.S.P.E.C.T...........79

Self Reflection

Section Four: Don't Get it Twisted............99

Self Reflection

Conclusion & Prayer

Thank You

To my mother who has been my number one supporter throughout my entire life. I have all of the best parts of you I am I forever grateful to God that He chose you to be my mom.

To my son, you are my biggest inspiration and my greatest accomplishment. Your life is just beginning. I thank God that He trusted 16 year old me to be your mom. Let Him lead. Lean not unto your own understanding. Trust Him.

To all of my family and friends who have loved me through my mess, never shamed me through my transition, and who walk through life with me on a daily basis.

To Miss Pam, thank you for believing in me and trusting me to teach the babies. For training me and for always having my back.

This book is dedicated to my best friend, Sharnita LaDawn Solomon, who left this earth too soon and who I miss every single day.

Foreword

Being a woman of God can be difficult, because being called to a higher standard requires hard work, discipline, and sacrifice. But through all of these things, and by living in obedience, we will have a greater reward for all eternity.

Trust me, I am talking to myself as I am talking to you. One thing I did not want to do is write a book to scare anyone or make them feel as if staying pure and living at an absolute standard of holiness is impossible when it is a goal that is completely attainable. I had to pray to God and ask Him exactly what He wanted me to say to you all. He said to write from exactly where I am, so, that is what I'm doing. Writing from a place of being in a healthy, functioning relationship that is not revolved around sex. Helping women live to the standard that God has called them to and to expose the lies of the enemy that try to keep us bound to sin and to our past.

When I first got the idea to write this book, it was almost four years ago and I was single with zero prospects, and it was a whole lot easier to keep it holy before I was dating. Although the subjects I talk about will still be the same, it will be coming from a different place of lé struggle. We will talk about being in a relationship God's way that is still full of love, passion and intimacy while still presenting ourselves as heirs to our Father's Kingdom.

Being royalty means carrying yourself in a manner in which your standards and what you claim to believe are evident in your life. Not because you go around talking about it, but because you live it, because the fruit of your life displays evidence. You have a different aura about you; you shine a light that only comes from living according to the Word of God. It is not about following a bunch of rules; it is about living within the boundaries that keep us safe.

So let's look at a few things to make sure we are conducting ourselves accordingly, projecting the correct message, and living as

daughters of the King…

Section One - Don't Believe the Hype

You are worthy.

Who are you? Sometimes that can be the most condescending question ever. Like, what do you mean who *am* I? I'm the daughter of the King! But really, is that our first response? If you're churchy, maybe, but for most of us it is not. That is because most times we forget ourselves *if* we even know at all. The real questions we should ask is not who am I, but who am I in Christ? Who has He called me to be? What does He require of me? What purpose did He create me for? Because at the end of the day, it is all about living out the purpose He placed us on earth for. And knowing our worth will keep us from making detrimental decisions that get us off course and off the narrow path. Knowing our worth keeps us from relationships that ruin our hearts and our spirits and keep us from the one God has for us.

Now this book is not about how to catch a man, but it is about being rooted authentically in who God has created you to be. And the bonus is that it will help you hold your stance as a queen so your king can recognize you. It is not your job to make a man *see* you. I have had many conversations with my married male friends and they all have told me similar things - this is what I have gathered. If a man wants you there is nothing that will keep him from pursuing you. You will not have to question his intentions and you will not wonder what space you fit in into his life. You know the quote "It doesn't take a whole day to recognize sunshine?" Well, it doesn't take men years to figure out if you are the one. And once they realize this, they will do what is necessary and take action. Therefore, we must have our standards set in order for a man to meet them, and when he wants you, he will do whatever it takes to meet those expectations. Not expectations that we have put on them, but how God expects His sons to treat His daughters. Because women cannot make men change, but a man will indeed make necessary adjustments to prove his love. Your standards will not be too high and you will not be too much for him to handle. You will be just enough for him. He will take on the challenge to grow. He will challenge you to grow. He will step up for a woman that he loves and he will do what it takes to win her. Most men love a challenge. They are innate hunters. They do not like things given too easily. So if a man is making excuses as to why he does not have time for you, why he can't commit to you, or pressing you into "proving" your love by expressing it sexually, NEXT. Nope, goodbye, see you later. It's time to move on.

I know this book is about sexual purity, but sidebar, knowing your worth is not just about snagging the right man, it rolls over into all aspects of life. Choosing the right career, attending the right school, and even having the right friends; how many of us have taken a job because we were either desperate for income or did not think we were qualified for something more? Were you someone who did not apply to an Ivy League or college at all because you did not think you would be able to keep up? And did you not have friends to encourage you to go for the higher position, start your own business, or apply to the school of your choice? But said things that would only confirm your doubt and play on your insecurities? So whether it is dating or making other life choices, knowing your worth and being grounded in who God has called you to be, will always ensure that you are putting yourself in the best position possible to succeed in whatever you are working to accomplish.

Okay, back to the script. One day I was watching one of those shows where people go around looking for valuable pieces to auction. A gentleman sold precious artifacts for a couple hundred bucks and the person he sold them to turned around and sold them for *thousands*. The man did not understand what he had, but if he would have realized what they were worth, then he would have treated them differently...better. A woman who does not understand that she is the prize and gives herself up too easily is like that precious artifact; especially if put into the hands of a man who does not know the true value in who he has.

I lived a long time not knowing or understanding my worth. Not because I was not taught or told, but because I was lacking a real and true relationship with the Lord Jesus Christ. I have a mother, grandparents, and aunts who would always affirm me. An amazing godfather who for a long time was my standard of what I wanted my husband to be like - and my standards are pretty high. He filled in the gap that my father left. He was my protector. He helped support me both emotionally and financially. He was my chef and my driver. He's the reason I love of The Three Stooges - watching it on Saturday mornings eating a yummy breakfast that he made. He was the one who scared the boys away. (He asked my 8th grade dinner dance date if he knew where the Quinnipiac River was and what cement shoes were, y'all - sorry Carlton.) But he did it driving us in his convertible Saab and I just thought I was too cute - he always made me feel like a princess. He was the one I was afraid to tell I was pregnant. His opinion of me mattered, and still does. But most importantly, he loves my godmother the way Christ loves the church. He would lay down his life for her. She has never wanted for anything. She's a boss, she can hold her own, but she does not have to. I always saw the way he loved her and I wanted my husband to be Just. Like. Him. He always made sure I felt loved and cared for. He always made sure I felt special. But the truth of the matter is, people can tell you every single day that you are beautiful or that you are worthy, but if you do not hear it from the One who created you, then there is no way that you will understand the depth of His love for you. You will then go seeking love and fulfillment in things and in men and you will give yourself away mentally, emotionally, and most importantly - spiritually.

When we lack spiritual maturity it puts us in a vulnerable position to be duped by the enemy's schemes. We are wide open and exposed to his fiery darts. We are unaware of the tricks he plays and the lies that he puts in our minds. It gives him an opportunity to play puppeteer with our emotions. He manipulates our minds and our actions. Don't get me wrong, he cannot make us do anything, but he does plant seeds that cause us to sin. He'll remind us of things we used to do. Things we love to do but know are not beneficial. Familiar things…

But before we set standards of what we require for our lives, we need to make sure we possess the things that attract the type of man we are looking for. Then, we can discern whether he was sent from God, or sent as a distraction.

If we take a look at our dating history, we often find that we tend to date the same man over and over - simply with a different face and name. We keep attracting the same type because we are not changing ourselves. We are holding on to old things. We have given ourselves away before the proper time and now have ungodly soul-ties and wonder why we just cannot seem to get it right. We have a string of heartbreaks and open wounds and we just do not know what to do or what we are doing wrong. So the question is what are the steps we need to take to heal those wounds and break the strongholds?

Step one: Pray.

I know that sounds simple, but if we really understood the spiritual attack that we were under on a daily basis, we could deduce how important prayer is for our lives. We are on a battlefield y'all. The devil wants to take us out and he wants to stifle any gift that we have inside of us that will advance our lives, bear fruit, and increase the kingdom of God. This is why spending time with God in prayer is important. Just as spending time with friends or your boyfriend creates closeness, relationship and intimacy; spending time with God in prayer does the same exact thing. When you spend time with Him you get to understand the way He communicates with YOU - not your momma or your grandma. You become more sensitive to the unctions of God. Your heart becomes softened and you can hear Him clearly. In prayer, your discernment increases because you become more connected to God's heart, and those "something told me's," you learn are prompts from the Holy Spirit. It is God telling you "he's not the one!" or "yes, this is it, now follow these instructions".

Prayer creates an intimacy with God and a friendship with Him so that when we are getting off track He can snatch us right on back. If our ears are open to listen to Him, it is easier to reel us in and set us back in the right direction. Prayer is not just spouting out a laundry list of things we need, it is thanking God for His goodness and of course making our requests known, but it is in the sitting and listening to what He has to say that creates the connection between us and God. And in that sweet spot where your heart is open and your mind is fixed on Him and your ears are tuned to His voice is where God can keep you from making mistakes that take you off course and away from the one He has for you. This does not mean that you will meet the love of your life on the first try and never break up - especially if you are a teen reading this. But even in relationships that end, God wants us to learn something from that person. Even if he is a Jesus loving, living man of God, he may not be the man of God for you. But again, you should always learn from these experiences. Things that will help you grow. Not things that will tear you down or make you feel worthless. So any relationship that is making you feel less than worthy is not ordained by God. The world will have us to believe that we have to learn through heartbreak. And although break ups hurt, it should never leave you heart wrenched for an extended period of time. You should never feel so low that you contemplate things such as suicide, never dating again, switching teams or causing harm to the other person…or their things. You give yourself a time limit, you cry; you whine to your friends, you go to the gun range and let off some steam, take a kickboxing class, whatever. But after that time, you get up, get your life together, give it to God and keep it pushing. Because living a life of holiness and having high standards will sometimes suck and when relationships end you may feel like your heart is broken & it's never going to mend. But one day, you'll see why God ended it and saved you from something that could have been detrimental to your life and your ministry. This is a lot easier when sex and soul ties are not involved but we'll get to that a little later.

Step two: Understand that God has a purpose for your life.

The devil is a liar. That is not just a churchy Christianese saying. It is the truth! He is a liar. He is the father of lies and he will do whatever it takes to make us believe that the things we've done wrong have disqualified us from running the race and from walking in the destiny God has for us. Don't believe the hype! He will plant seeds of doubt and shame that will make us shrink back so that we never fulfill our purpose. Then, the people who were supposed to be healed by our testimonies will never get to hear them because we sat on our gifts in the name of fear which is straight up disobedience. He would love for us to sit in that sin place of rebellion even if we are unknowingly there - *especially* if we are unknowingly there. This is why prayer and hearing from God is key. When our hearts are locked with God's, we can decipher His voice from the voice of the enemy. We are not as easily deceived because we know the truth of God's Word and we can compare what we are hearing to what God says. And no matter what you have gone through, no matter what your past looks like, He can still use you to bring glory to His kingdom and there is nothing the devil can do to stop it.

I use to pose for men's magazines, never nude, but close enough to not bring glory to the kingdom of God; showing the public things that were meant for my husband's eyes only. But even then, there were things I would not do. No spread eagle, no thongs. My bits were always covered. As low as that standard was, it was still a standard and whenever I had a photo shoot, the stylist would always adhere to it. One time, I was shooting a music video and the assistant director said "You can turn around & dance with your butt facing the camera" (I had on shorts) I politely said "No I cannot" - there were some things I just was not having *lé shrug* I always got called back to work again. I say all that to say, I knew God then, well I knew of God. I went to church, sat on the pew with my great grandmother's name on it, I had the same Sunday school teacher that my mother once had and who my son would one day have. I participated in the Girls Friendly Society on Tuesdays after school, and went to Episcopal Camp every summer. So I had a foundation, but it was not firm. I did not *know* God, I did not have a relationship with Him. He was the Big Guy in the sky that I did not want to get upset because I knew He was watching. I did not know Him deeply... intimately. But the little bit of Him that I had on the inside is what unknowingly gave me those standards. People would always tell me I was different, that I carried myself differently than other girls I worked with on set. And that there was something about me that they knew couldn't be messed with - it was the calling on my life. He let me get in just enough to give me a platform to be able to use in the future but He never let me get in too deep. I did not know it then, but I was called for His purpose. He chose me; a teen mom was called to minister to young women and mentor teenage girls. *insert upside down emoji face*

One day when I became an adult I remembered being nine years old, sitting on that pew with Nana McCoy's name on it, looking at the stained glass windows of St. Luke's Church and hearing a voice say "You are special". It was audible. It was clear. I did not know what that was then but when I got the revelation a few years ago, I tell you this, the tears could not stop flowing. That was the voice of God. He was letting me know that I was special to Him and that He loved me. That He would never leave me nor forsake me, and that He was with me and that He would be with me forever. No matter what I did, no matter what I was going to do, I was special to Him. And through all of my mishaps He would still use me to bring glory to and increase His Kingdom. He would grow me up into a woman who had high standards for her life and for the man who would one day be my covering and the covering for our household. God wants the same for you beautiful woman reading this book. He wants your standards to be His standards. And just like that assistant director on set, a man will see that your standards are in place and that you are unwavering in your convictions. He will then rise to meet them, or step off.

Step three: Study.

How can we hear God's voice if we do not know what He says? Studying the word of God helps us to understand Him. How He talks, what He thinks about us, and how He deals with us —

even in our disobedience. How can we know that the devil is a liar if we don't even know what he is lying about? If we do not know that we were fearfully & wonderfully made in the image of God. That we are the apple of His eye, and that He wants to bless us exceedingly abundantly above. If we do not know what God's word says, then we can never fully walk in our purpose because we will only be leaning on our own understanding. We will not know to speak these things over our lives and to decree and to declare them over ourselves. Our words are powerful and the things we think and the things we speak over ourselves have the ability to change our lives. We have to speak God's word over ourselves on a daily basis to remind us of who we are in Christ. If we are not continually studying the word we will not know that His ways are not like our ways and that His thoughts are far above our thoughts.

That means we have to read the word to know the word. So when He asks us to do something that may seem ridiculous, we will do it because we want to forever be in obedience. Then, if God says to not give that six-figure fine man the time of day, but go with this man who is just starting his business and is barely making ends meet, you will listen because you know that God knows something that you do not. Meanwhile, the world will be looking at you like you just grew a foot out of your forehead. But what we don't know is that the six-figure dude has made a living for himself but he did it without God so it will not last, or he has an incurable STD, or he is a womanizer. But the other man is honest, God is in every step of his plan, therefore, whether he becomes a millionaire or not, he will still be a success. He will be a man who will know how to cover your home in prayer and your children will be blessed because they have a father who knows *the Father.* God wants His best for us. And sometimes we look at what is happening on the outside of a person while God is looking at their heart. He knows what is happening on the inside and He sends us flags, signals and signs saying NO but we get so caught up in the natural and pay no attention to what is going on in the spiritual.

The Bible is the blueprint to what we should look for when a man is trying to date or court us. Does he know God's word? Does he study to show himself approved? Does he have the fruit of the Spirit? Is he kind? How does he treat the waiter or better yet, the homeless person on the street who can do nothing for him? Is he gentle and does he have self-control with you or does he feel like he has to yell, use force or put his hands on you to get his way? How does he show love that has nothing to do with sex? Is his heart full of joy and peace and goodness, or is he always mad, mean or rude? How is he when something goes wrong - can he handle pressure? Is. He. Faithful. In all things.

This is why reading God's word is so important. It is a constant reminder of what He wants for our lives. The bible is God's love letter to us. It is what He left so that we would know Him - intimately.

We have to continually speak God's word over our lives in our prayer time. No one can ever lie to you about who you are if you understand how the King sees you - as His daughter, His princess.

Step four: Apply.

Faith, the substance of things hoped for, the evidence of things not seen. What good is it to study God's word if we do not apply it? The devil does not care if we go to church, he does not even care if we read our bibles. He cares when we start applying what we know of God & His word to our lives. When we begin to walk in the power that God has given us, the devil begins to tremble in his stanky little boots.

I am doing a Bible study right now by Priscilla Shirer called *Armor of God*. This week we are studying the shield of faith. And in today's lesson the meaning of faith hit me over the head like a tons of bricks! Paul said to "take up" your shield (of faith). That requires action, which requires us to move. That means that when things come our way, like those flaming darts of the enemy, our faith in God helps us to stand firm and extinguish them. Sometimes a fiery dart comes wrapped in a package that you have always wanted. Tall, dark, and handsome or short, yellow, and round - whatever your flavor is; the devil does not show up in a red cape wielding a pitch fork. He shows up in everything you have ever wished for. Things you may have wanted, but did not necessarily need in your life. Therefore, we must have our shields erect to block out the things that are not meant for us.

Faith is like winter gear. It is a safeguard that shields us from the elements. For the majority of my life I had to endure the brutal winters of Connecticut. When I was a child, my mom and I caught the city bus for many of those years. Not just in the summer months, but year round, and that meant walking from our home to the bus stop to then stand there and pray that the bus came on time. We had to bundle up in hats, gloves, scarves, thermals, two pair of socks, winter coats *with* the hoods over our hats. Although we could still feel a bit of the zero below air, our winter gear made it so that we were protected from the winds, frostbite and head colds. What good would it be if we had all of that gear and left it at home in the coat closet? What if we walked outside wearing nothing but our jeans and sweaters, without picking up the things that would protect us from being exposed to the elements? The very things that can keep you from freezing to death, or at the very least, save your fingertips and toes from freezing over. Faith is our protection and it does us no good if we do not pick it up and use it. What good is a shield if it is left along the wayside looking pretty collecting dust? Like Scripture says, weapons will form but they shall not prosper, and they cannot prosper because our faith in God will keep us on the path to our destiny. When He calls us to do something, move somewhere, or speak to someone, no matter how crazy it may seem, we will do it because we know that God has something for us on the other side. We know that the person we talked to will be blessed because of our obedience. Being obedient to God unlocks blessings and abundance, not because we are being rewarded for our actions, but because God knows that He can trust us with what has been given.

What does this last section about faith have to do with knowing your worth? Well, if we do not pray, if we do not study, if we do not understand our purpose, then how can we possibly have the faith to apply them? How can we have faith that God will send the one who will love us just as we are? Without faith, we lack the confidence of who we are in Christ and our identity becomes severely skewed. Without faith, we will stay in a bad relationship too long; we will take a lot from a person who does not deserve us and we will give ourselves away, sexually, because we will think that that is what we have to do to keep him. Then, we begin to damage ourselves emotionally as well as spiritually. When we do not apply the word of God to our lives, everything we read is pretty much null & void. The devil does not care if we pray or go to church. He cares if we apply what we are being taught to our everyday lives. He does not care if we are reading the Word, but he cares if we are applying the principles and values of God that keep us from sinning. Sin keeps us away from God. It keeps us from speaking to God because of guilt and shame. And the farther away from God we get, the easier it is for the slithery snake to slide right in. We will see red flags, but because we are so disconnected from God, we are not convicted in a way that we once were or would be if we were spending time with Him. We forget who and Whose we are and we begin to believe the lies of the enemy. We begin to believe that we are unworthy of someone who will treat us like the princesses He created by His design. Without faith in who God has called us to be, we begin to believe the hype that we will never be good enough and that there couldn't possibly be someone out there who lives for God and who wants to love us like Christ loves the church.

As high as the bar is that my godfather set, it pales in comparison to knowing the bar that my Daddy in heaven has set. God wants you to know Him and to understand just how much He loves and cares for you. He wants you to know how precious and amazing you are. He is our Dad. And He left us His word so that we would know just how much we should think of ourselves. So if you did not have a daddy in the flesh to tell you just how precious you are, He made sure you were covered in that area. Before you were placed in your mother's womb He left provision through the Holy Bible. But we have to pick it up and read it to know just who it is that He has called us to be. He does not want us to give ourselves away easily. He wants us to be aware of our worth. Just like the man who sold the artifacts for thousands, he was aware of their value when the other man was not, and moved on the opportunity to acquire the property. We are not property, but we are a prized possession. So don't mess around with jokers who do not understand your worth when there is a man out there who will pick you up when a fool has put you down. When there is a man ready to treat you like *a daughter of the King…*

Self Reflection

Here are a few questions to think about. If you cannot answers these right now, it's okay. But go back & fill them in once you have prayed on it & have gotten revelation from God. Use a notebook or journal if you need more room.

Who am I in Christ?

Who has He called me to be?

What purpose did He create me for?

What does He require of me?

Section two - Keep it Tight

Purity.

Is being abstinent easy? No! Heck no! Especially when you are dating someone who you are extremely attracted to. When God first gave me the idea for this book I was not dating. It was just me and God. I was very focused on my relationship with Him and dating was on the back burner until I truly understood who I was in this new found role...abstinent until marriage. It was very easy to keep my legs closed when there was no one I wanted to get between them. When there isn't a prospect in sight and you can keep your sole focus on God. But it is a very different thing to have someone who is consistently in your life. Someone showing interest and that interest turns into hanging out, and that hanging out turns into dating and getting to know one another and dating turns into courting and having intention of moving your relationship towards marriage. Then that person is making you feel special, and that making you feel special turns into to wanting to willingly open those legs. That is not a *terrible* thing. Sex is an expression of our love and the way we show our feelings for someone we care about. It is the way God set us up. But that is to be done under His covenant of marriage and not a boyfriend/girlfriend situation. God knows that we are going to get to the point in our relationship where we want to show that expression. Once it is beyond mere lust. Once you are attracted to them beyond what you see on the outside. Once their heart and mind attracts you. Once you are completely and utterly in love with their soul. *That's* when it gets tricky, that is when a goodnight kiss in the car turns into you straddled across their lap like "oh, how'd I get here". But that is when you have to pray your strength and keep your eyes fixed on God. I know this is going to sound cliché, but you have to pray yo' strength and you have to die to your flesh. I am not speaking to you from a place where I have not been and still currently am. This is my precise location at this very moment as I type this and I am not telling you to do things that I am not doing myself. I know God wants me to write this book while I am still unmarried but dating because it is very easy to say, as a married woman or a woman with no boo, just pray and it will be okay. But me telling you this standing in the same spot that you are or will be at some point, I hope will help you to take heed and find relief in the fact that it *is* possible to be in a relationship and keep it holy until marriage - if marriage is the goal. Not everyone wants to or will be married and that's okay. And to those who will argue and say that one should be able to have sex and not marry, I am not God and you don't have to answer to me. Consult Him about that and know that you are in fact living in sin. And as believers we are supposed to live according to God's Word which says to wait.

Anywho, there are some people who have committed their lives to Christ and not having sex ever or ever again is A-okay. They have made a commitment and doing the work of the Lord is more important than having an orgasm. Not to minimize what sex is, but sex outside of covenant is purely for one's own pleasure. It does not glorify God. It is self-seeking. Having sex outside of marriage can multiply, but that often leads to more broken homes and single parents families. Where sex in a marriage is worship unto the Lord and has a better chance at providing a loving healthy environment for the children it produces.

One thing I have to always keep in the front of my mind is the calling and the mantle that God has placed on my life. You have to remember that no man (or boy) is worth aborting the destiny that God has for you. You have to say to yourself "self, what it is God is requiring me to do, and how will having sex outside of covenant affect my witness?" "How will this affect the authenticity of the ministry that He put inside of me?" God has called me to preach purity and to show women and girls that it is indeed possible to have a successful courtship. A courtship that is full of intimacy without having sex and tying yourself to that person prematurely. How would I make God look if I'm out here in the streets having sex? Because what is done in the dark will come to light and God *will* expose you. Not to embarrass you, but to heal you in that area and to always make sure that His word is going forth in truth. This is not to say that we cannot mess up, have a weak moment, or go a little too far. God gives us grace. *Thanks God.* But He will not allow you (me) to live in a place of sin while preaching His word. He will not allow me to be a hypocrite. He has given me a mission to show that purity is possible and that you do not have to have sex to make a man fall in love with you. Sex does not make anyone fall in love and sex sure enough won't keep a man that doesn't want to be kept. Without love and commitment, it only curbs the appetite for lust, and that is a temporary fulfillment.

The world is set up to make people believe that it is okay to sleep around and go on about your business. But guess what? It is not about our business, it is about our Father's business, and that business is to spread the gospel, not our legs before "I do". How can we effectively share God's Word if we are living in sin? We cannot. But how do we effectively live a life of holiness in the world today? Where do we start? How do we keep it together? That is when accountability kicks in.

There is no way to be in the struggle alone, especially when you have already experienced sex, and good sex at that. You must have people you can trust and that you can rely on. You need people who will not judge you when you mess up, because you may stumble while on this journey of abstinence. And you do not need someone who is going to scold you but love you and help you walk through. You will need someone you can call who will pray with you not shame you. With that being said, it is important to be honest with your accountability and tell them *before* it happens. Like, when it's getting too hot or you know it's getting too late and you feel like you should leave. OR just tell them you are going to be at your boyfriend's house and you need them to check in periodically. Because in all reality, once it's hot, it's hard to stop. But if they know beforehand, then they can check in and check up on you - keep your ringer on. If you are not honest with your accountability partners, then there is no point of having them. Even if we try to hide it, God will always give us a way out. Sometimes He will have to use that ram in the bush... One night a friend purse-dialed me.. twice, and I could hear her conversation. I heard "but if I go to your place..." I hung up, and texted her "GO HOME". She called immediately and wondered how I knew what she was thinking about doing - going to his house and putting herself in a compromising position. She thought the Lord put it on my heart, lol. It wasn't that deep, but He did have her purse dial me and I ear-hustled. I am saying all that to say, it is important for you to have people who will help keep you in check. I did not judge her, or scold or talk down "how could you even think to go over..." no, we laughed about it and she nicknamed me her ram in the bush.

Here's the thing, we are not perfect beings we are going to take a misstep, we are going to fall, and we are going to get back up start all over again. When God first shut my sex life down I tried to obey immediately but I messed up... a few times. It took time, prayer, discipline, and accountability to get to the point where I am today. Where I want to have sex, but I will not because I know that it will put me ten steps back. But when I had gone too far, I got my life together - and quickly. Because living in disobedience will put me in a place where I cannot fully reach my potential and it will take me off track. It will knock me off the course that God has for my life and I will not be able to fulfill the destiny that He has for me.

Like I said before, God will expose hypocrites. One, I am not a hypocrite. I remember when I got to the point where I knew God was calling me to teach Sunday school. But I had no idea He was calling me to mentor the teen girls. And for me to teach God's word in truth, I knew my life had to be in order. I did not volunteer until I knew that I was steady in my walk and solid in keeping my body holy and committed to Him. Two, I don't like being embarrassed. So to think of being put on blast for saying one thing and doing another, ay yi yi, it freaks me out! But the more I committed myself to God fully, the closer I got to Him, and the more I saw that the intimacy I thought I had in dating relationships before was a facade. The more He began to expose the counterfeit factors in my life and over the years, He has allowed me to see just what He kept me from. Keeping my body holy and committed to the Lord has given me a sense of peace that I have never had before. I am not worrying if my monthly will be here. I am not worried about STDs. And when relationships end, they are not as heart wrenching because we have not tied our souls together. There is no ripping or tearing because we did not create a bond that was not meant to be broken.

God does not ask us to wait until marriage to have sex as a punishment but as protection. Keeping yourself pure gives you a sense of freedom not bondage as the world would like to portray. They would like for you to think that waiting until marriage is out of date, but the word of God is *never* out of date and it will forever be the standard for what is right and what is true. So don't let the world fool you into thinking that in order to be successful in a relationship that sex has to be involved - it does not. People will talk about you, they will say things like "well I know *he* ain't waiting" they will try to discourage you and tear you down. But that is the work of the enemy and it is his way of keeping you in bondage with an illusion of freedom. He tries to mask it as self-expression, owning one's body, not letting society tell them what to do with their bodies. That's a bunch of malarkey. We are not our own. We were bought with a price. And we are to keep ourselves holy and committed to the Lord who died for us.

When we give our lives to Christ, and decide to follow His word, and are baptized with the Holy Spirit, we now have God living on the inside of us. That means, whatever we go through, He goes through. So essentially when we have sex before marriage, an act that He wants us to wait to experience, we are now raping the Holy Spirit. Ah! It sounds crazy when you think of it that way. I remember I the first time I heard my pastor say that - it broke my heart to think about how I had done that. It sounds brutal and harsh. But when we have sex before marriage we are putting our bodies through brutal and harsh conditions. We are giving away pieces of ourselves to a person who has not committed himself to us. And often times we are looking for love, seeking attention and affection from someone who is not even emotionally ready or available to give their heart to you. They just want to whet their physical appetite.

But ladies, this is not a game. Just as we do not want men playing with our emotions, we cannot use this as a form of manipulation either. Your heart and mind both need to be in the right place. This is not about getting a husband; it is about your commitment to God and making a covenant with Him. To live for Him - mind, body and soul until you create a covenant with the one God has for you.

Sex is so powerful which is why it is so perverted in the world. It is beautiful. It is two souls becoming one and making a covenant with God. It brings forth life. It is worship to God under the covenant of marriage. And the world tries to turn it into a sick and twisted thing that makes people feel as though it is a shameful act. Sex is not and should not be synonymous with shame and it should never be thought of as a taboo subject. Sex should be talked about in church. Because if we were educated about sex properly in the first place, then maybe it would not be so abused and used in the wrong manner in the world. Church should be your safe space and your refuge to discuss anything.

Once you are in a serious relationship it is important to have a church family, not to be in your business, but to help hold you accountable. A few years ago the man I was dating got us tickets for the Bad Boy concert…in Las Vegas. Honestly, I was a wee bit nervous to be alone…in a hotel…with my boo. But a friend of mine, a married friend, sends me a text one day saying that she and her husband were coming along with us to Vegas in an effort to help keep us holy. She did not ask me, she *told* me. And I was not mad, not one bit. And if it were the other way around I would have done the same. You have to have people around you who are going to help you keep your life together, or, your legs. We cannot put ourselves in compromising positions and think that we are so strong that we can resist the temptation…we cannot. Well, we can, but only for so long. So if you know that being at his house late at night or being alone period is a problem, then you will have to make a choice to not be over there all times of night. Or maybe you can only go on group dates. You will have to make a decision and stick to it. Some of you reading this are probably like "Ugh, this is so much work". Yes, anything worth having is worth working for. That is not just for careers and material possessions but for relationships and our bodies too. You will not just haphazardly keep it together and you cannot do it alone. You have to work hard for it. You cannot just blindly play it by ear and think that you will be successful - you won't be. And you won't be unsuccessful because you don't want to be, but because you have not put the proper precautions in place. It takes intentional living to keep it together and not succumb to the temptation. It takes effort. As with anything else in life that is to be done in excellence to make sure that we are living our best life possible. We tend to work hard at other aspects of our lives, but fail to work hard at the things that matter most. It is easier to give ourselves away in hopes of finding true love. We don't think it should be "this hard" to live a life in accordance to what God sees as best for us but will have no problem working hard for a job, a degree, or a car that will do little to nothing to move us forward in our purpose and prepare for eternity. The ideas of marriage, relationships and sex have become so skewed by the world. We act like having sex before marriage is normal and that waiting for marriage is obscene. It's screwed up and backwards and I thank God that he has given me revelation on why I need to stay holy and pure until my wedding night. I am so happy that He gave me revelation on how sex outside of marriage affects me not only spiritually but physically too.

If you notice in the word, Paul stayed warning the church about premature sexual relations *"Run from sexual sin! No other sin so clearly affects the body as this one does. For sexual immorality is a sin against your own body. Don't you realize that your body is the temple of the Holy Spirit, who lives in you and was given to you by God? You do not belong to yourself, for God bought you with a high price. So you must honor God with your body."* 1 Corinthians 6:18-20 NLT. Sex is the only sin that *clearly affects* the body. This means that the effects are evident, visible - you can take that as you wish

And as one of my girlfriends pointed out, sex is the only sin that becomes not a sin as soon as you are married. Once you are in covenant you can get it poppin' whenever you want. Sex is the trickiest sin so you know it has to be important. And like I said before, The Holy Spirit is in you, and we are dragging Him into our mess. And as I have said in one of my blogs, Runnnnnn!!!! Run! Run! Run! We can try little tricks like wearing granny panties or not waxing, it does not work, trust me. You need to be committed to God. You need people to hold you accountable.

This life is not one to be lived alone. We need community. If you are the type of person who does not like people questioning you or does not like to have people in your business, then most likely, you will fail - in whatever it is you are trying to accomplish. And because sex is so powerful, the devil loves to manipulate it and loves for us to think that giving ourselves away all willy nilly is all right. Keeping our bodies pure is not just a gift for our husbands, but it is a gift to us.

Keeping our bodies holy and pure is a freedom like no other. Ladies, if you are reading this book and you have been sexually active in the past then you know the worry of "oh no, my period is late" or "what's that itch". Now imagine, every month knowing that your monthly will arrive and that that itch may only mean that you're a little sweaty and you just need a shower? People in the world make it seem as though keeping our bodies pure is old fashioned and out of date. But peep what Paul says in 1 Thessalonians 4:2-5 (NLT)

"For you remember what we taught you by the authority of the Lord Jesus. God's will is for you to be holy, so stay away from all sexual sin. Then each of you will control his own body and live in

holiness and honor— not in lustful passion like the pagans who do not know God and his ways." That is New Testament, so if we are truly followers of Christ, then this is the way that we ought to live. We have to have self-control in all aspects of life - including keeping our privates to ourselves before the appropriate time. This is not an old fashioned concept as the world would have us to believe. They would love for us to accept the fact that we are living in bondage when in reality it is the ultimate freedom. No worrying about unplanned pregnancies, STDs or soul ties.

Way back in the Bible days folks did not have the wedding ceremonies we have today. To be considered married, the two became one when they had sex and their souls were tied together under God. They were now husband & wife. Their *souls* were *tied* and the two became *one*.

We are nothing but souls that were given flesh and bones to walk this earth to glorify and to add to God's kingdom. That is all we are! But that is a *big* deal. So our souls being connected and intertwined with people before it is time, before they are our husband only brings about heartache, pain and unnecessary things to deal with when you do become married. It not only binds you to that person, but to all of the people that they have been with. I have my own crazy and I do not need your crazy ex-girlfriend hopping into my spirit too. No thanks. So this is why keeping our bodies pure is a gift to ourselves, as well as our future husbands.

Self Reflection

What it is that God is calling me to do?

Are there soul ties you need to break? What are they? Who are they with?

How does having premarital sex influence the effectiveness of a person's ministry? (Answer from what you have witnessed or experienced personally.)

Section three - R.E.S.P.E.C.T.

Self-Respect.

When we give ourselves away to a man too quickly, often times, it causes them to lose respect. Because when sex is given without commitment most men now feel that their goal was achieved and can now move on to the next woman. And on the contrary, in our minds, we think that this is the way to win them and to show them that we care. They lose interest and we get attached. Our minds are wired differently.

Am I saying that having sex before marriage means you do not have any self-respect, no, not at all. But many times when we have sex too early it causes men to see us differently. Again, I have talked to a few men about this and they have all said something similar and it may be something about their scientific make up (don't quote me on that), but they said it is like a switch goes off and they literally see women differently when they give it up too soon. That is *super* whack, I know, but I think that it is valuable information to have.

I am fully aware that having self-respect should have nothing to do with a man but, this book is in fact about sex so stating facts about how men are wired is indeed important. Should the men be held accountable, of course, but I am writing to you about having standards and conducting ourselves as daughters of the King. The truth is, I did not respect myself enough to hold a man to a standard. I did think that sex was what I had to do in order for him to love me. Time and time again. Failed relationship after failed relationship.

It was not until I saw myself as worthy, knew who I was in Christ, and had the respect for myself that I was truly able to be open enough to date and fall in love with someone who would love me through anything. And although our relationship did not lead to marriage, we can both say that it was the most functional, healthy relationship either of us has ever had.

The world likes us to believe that people should love us just the way we are and have respect for us no matter what we act like. But the truth is, a man is going to respect you as much as you respect yourself. Men can smell low self-esteem from a mile away. So where a good man will lift you up out of that place, a man seeking to take advantage will manipulate you and use you to get what they want and then bounce. Having respect for yourself will help the heartbreaks become few and far between. And this goes back to identity and truly understanding who you are.

When you are aware of your place in God's family, a royal heir to the throne, a princess in His Kingdom, you will exude a confidence that will attract the right people in your life. You will attract men who are serious about their business and their intentions with you. All of the jokers will step off and be weeded out. They will not even come near you because they know that you are not one to be fooled with. They know that they cannot get over on you and that you are not the one to play games with. Having self-respect is a shield for foolywags and you will begin to notice that you're dealing with a lot less drama. They will have to move to the side because God's imprint will be written all over your life. So when you begin to feel down or feel like you need to give a man your body, or dress too sexy for attention, just know that the Lord may just be hiding you for the right one who will seek God and find you hiding in Him.

I remember a time when I would be out with my girlfriends and they all would be getting hit on and it was like I was invisible. I was like "wait; hold up, I'm here too!" This can begin to bring up much insecurity. You may have doubts about this new found life in Christ if you are a new believer. Wondering if you should go back to the old ways where you received lots of attention. But old ways do not open new doors. And the fact of the matter was, I was not dressing any differently or acting much differently. I was always the sober one in the club before I really knew Christ. I like to go out and dance but I was not a big clubber. I had to be dragged out for appearances when I worked on the television show Wild N' Out on MTV. I was loving, kind, gentle, and patient. I possessed *most* of the fruits of the Spirit before I knew what they were. So I was like dang God, what is happening? Why is no one trying to holla? The reality was, although I was the same on the outside, there was something immensely different exuding from the inside of me. Something I could not see, but others could feel. The Holy Spirit was alive on the inside of me and people could sense it …and I stopped cussin'.

A few years later I was talking to one of my sisters in Christ and she was saying the same thing. How she would be out and all of her friends would be getting hit on and she would be sitting there like "hello, I'm here too". She is *gorgeous* y'all - inside and out. As we were chatting we realized that we were not being ignored, God was hiding us. He had a shield over us and no fool off the street was going to be able to get to His precious daughter.

It is hard out here, trust me, I know it is. Because we are constantly seeing images online, on social media of women exposed, half dressed and that is what, to the naked eye, looks like is winning. But in all actuality, it is just for show. It's for likes and followers and it breeds false attention. It is not real. It is a facade. It's an artificial sense of self confidence. Once you are in a covenant with your husband it's all good. You can be as sexy as you want to be for him. That sexiness is not for the public or for your boyfriend. It is not for the whole world to see. It is not to be put on display. That is not what God created your body for. They do not need to see it all. They do not deserve to see it all. They did not make a commitment to you. You are precious and valuable; therefore, they do not deserve the prize that is *you* without a covenant. They don't deserve your mind, your heart, your spirit -

everything that comes along with giving them your body. Having sex is not just intercourse. Do not let the world dumb down just how powerful sex is. You are not just giving them a piece of you - but all of you. You are giving over all parts of you. You are exchanging bodily fluids and are committing an act that is making you become one before its time. That is contradictory to the way God created it to be once you commit your life to follow Him.

What I am saying is not the popular opinion but hey, what Jesus preached was not either and I am a disciple of His. Modesty is sexy. You can be modest and fly. You do not have to dress like someone's grandma covered from your chin to your ankles in order to look decent.

So be encouraged. If you are reading this book and you are transitioning to a life that is truly lived for Christ, you are not alone. You are not suddenly unattractive. You are covered by God until He sends the one who is going to be your earthly covering. There will be men that will fall out of your life and that is perfectly fine. If they fall away then they were no good in the first place. People are going to be mad. Friends may mock you. But guess what? People hated Jesus so they are going to hate you too. Or hate this new choice to live your life according to His word. People will call you corny and talk behind your back. But when they see your life prospering and being in love with a man who loves you to your core, they will be wanting some of what you have - Jesus.

Self Reflection

If you are sexually active, do you find yourself having sex before you are ready as a way to "get" a man (boy) to love you?

Do you feel like you can "fall in love" without sex? Why or Why not?

Do you feel like you can be in a relationship without sex?

Are you afraid of losing your boyfriend when you commit your body to Christ?

Section four - Don't Get it Twisted

There is no condemnation.

Therefore, there is now no condemnation for those who are in Christ Jesus, because through Christ Jesus the law of the Spirit who gives life has set you free from the law of sin and death.
Romans 8:1-2

When I first began teaching children's church, people judged me. Not to my face, but I heard what they had to say about me. Even though it hurt my feelings I did not let that stop me from doing what the Lord had called me to do. Because they had no idea what God was doing on the inside of me and the changes that He was making, the conviction He put on my heart, and just how seriously I was taking my walk and how committed I was to doing it "right." Living holy, being a woman of my word, and teaching from a place of authenticity and purity of heart. I wanted the Word of God to come straight from the Father to the babies with no residue of my past coming through.

Many people like to judge your life either by what they know of you or what they *think* they know of you. What people knew of me was that I was a teenage mother, a Wild 'N Out Girl, who was on the cover of *KING* magazine in a bathing suit with water dripping down my body from a water hose and that I used to star in music videos. They did not know my heart and they had no idea that even when I was in that world, I still had standards and that God had shielded me from many things that went on behind the scenes. They had no idea of the calling and the destiny that He had for my life. They had no idea that God was going to use all of that to reach His people. That He was going to use me in a mighty way. Even after I was half naked in public, He would use me to write a book on purity and keeping ourselves holy. God got jokes, but He knew what would happen all along.

Whether you are a born again virgin or a virgin in real time, people are going to judge your life. But we cannot let that get to us. If I had let other people's opinions get the best of me, I would be out of line and I would not be walking in my calling. I would be out of position and the people that I have been called to reach would not be reached…not by me anyway. But how do we live boldly in our present if our past is a bit checkered? How do we not let shame hold us back? How do we let go of fear of what others say or think about us? It may not be easy, but commit your life to Christ and forget about what the haters have to say about you. That is exactly what I did. We cannot let the opinions of others overtake us and scare us from fervently pursuing purpose. Romans 8:1-2 says it plainly and I took that scripture at its word. There is *no* condemnation once you are in Christ and I am in Him and His Spirit is in me, therefore, everything I did in my past was cast into the sea of forgetfulness. But I did have to make sure I was keeping my commitment to Christ and was living for Him fully. There were people I had to get rid of, jobs I could not take, and environments that I could no longer be in. And you know what, after a while, I did not miss any of it and would be uncomfortable now if I ever had to be there again. It would literally irritate my spirit because the Holy Spirit now resides inside of me and I am no longer able to be in environments that are not edifying.

We cannot say that we want to live for Christ but then go back to our old ways. But let's be honest, the moment you commit your life to Christ often times you will, as seasoned saints say, backslide. And guess what, that is where His grace will cover us. If you are someone who lived a life where you regularly had sex with your boyfriend then giving it up will be hard in the beginning. You may have a slip-up or two or seven, but that does not mean that God is mad at you or that you can no longer live your life in purity with your body committed to Him. It is just going to take more work than someone who has never had sex but it is indeed possible. You should never beat yourself up or think that you are a failure because you made a mistake. God loves us unconditionally and He does not look at us the way the world does. He does not shun us the moment we make a mistake. If your heart is submitted to Him, and you repent and turn away from that thing that keeps you bound to sin, He will forgive you and wipe your slate clean. He will toss your sin into the sea of forgetfulness and allow you to walk forward with no condemnation. But even in His forgiveness, do not frustrate His grace.

People like to use the grace that God gives freely as a "get out of jail free" card or a better term, get into bed free. But that is not what His grace is for. It is for blunders, slip ups, whatever you want to call it, because we are no longer bound to the law. But we cannot choose to live a lifestyle of sin and just expect His grace to cover it. That is not what it is there for and after a while, He will lift that grace and expose us, especially if you are in a position of leadership. He does not do that because He hates you, like said before, He does it because He loves you, wants you to receive healing in that area, and to make sure that His word is going forth in truth.

Maintaining a level of purity while still creating intimacy is tricky but it is possible and we cannot fall into the trap of taking that intimate place too far. We cannot knowingly "fall" into sin over and over again and count on God's grace and His mercy. Because the truth of the matter is, once you know what God's word says, you are held accountable for your actions and are open to judgement. You will begin to see that things you got away with before, you will no longer be able to get away with. You are now a disciple of Christ and you are a representative of Him. You are called to a higher standard. And you know the speech most of our parents gave us before we went out in public. You know the one where we were told not to act a fool. Not to touch nothin' or even look in that direction. Our parents would tell us for our protection, but also for us not embarrass them because we are a reflection of their parenting. God is not going to have us out in these streets making Him look crazy. He will snatch us back if we get too far out of line. He will remove the obstacle that is getting in the way of us walking fully in our calling. He will not allow us to live a double life. So no, there is no condemnation, but we have to do our best to live the life that God has called us to live. It is for His glory. It is for our protection.

Lastly, another way we can condemn ourselves is by comparing our lives with others. People love to boast about their highlight reel but never want to talk about their failed practice drills. Some folks love to brag about things that should really be an expectation if you are unmarried. One that I see quite often is people bragging on things that should be standard in one's life - things such as "28 with no kids" uh, okay? But how many abortions have you had? Maybe by the grace of God your sin was never made public and you really have not ever been pregnant. But how many STDs have you had? How many broken hearts because you had a premature soul tie? People love to condemn others and put each other down but have their own things in the closet that they can be judged for. Our God is a God of no condemnation. People in the world will judge and people in the church will judge because everyone is going to have an opinion about something. But our God is a God of forgiveness, He is a God of redemption, so do not let anyone else's accomplishments or what may seem to be accomplishments make you feel less than or unworthy and full of shame.

Shame is the thing that can trip us up. When we are remorseful about our pasts, and are not able to speak and live and move forward, it is usually because shame is holding us back. We are ashamed to say that we are now living this life in Christ because we are concerned about what people are going to say. We are concerned about the people who are going to try to bring things we use to do to make our new walk null and void. But they cannot do that. They can talk all they want but they cannot disrupt the call that God has on our lives if we are in Him, seeking Him, and being obedient to what He has called us to do. We have to understand that once we are in Him, old things are passed away and He does not condemn us, therefore we cannot let others condemn us and we cannot condemn ourselves - although that is what we tend to do.

It may not be someone else putting us down, sometimes we put our own selves down. We judge ourselves and we do not truly believe that we can do what God is asking of us because of things we did in the past. We are so ashamed, we are so hurt and embarrassed by former actions that we do not step out into the place that God is calling us to be in now. We are not bold enough because we are hidden behind that shame, fear and regret - all of the things that hold us back. Colossians 3:3 says that you have died and are now hidden in Christ. That old person is dead and the only place we should be hidden is behind Him.

We cannot live in a place of fear but we often do and we do not fully walk in our purpose because we are afraid of what we think about ourselves. We have not convinced ourselves that we are worthy. So many times it may not even be outside sources - it may be us. We are the ones condemning ourselves. We are the ones holding our own selves back. We are the ones holding ourselves to a standard that does not apply to our lives. So we need to get that together and be bold enough to walk in our purpose with our head held high. Because God loves us and He forgives us and He can use everything we have done for His glory once we are committed and submitted to Him.

From me being a teenage mother to being on the cover of *KING* half naked. No one can ever throw that in my face because I am bold enough to talk about the things that I have done. When we are open and honest it takes away the power. It takes away the enemy's ability to use our indiscretions. When we try to hide things is when it can be so easily used against us to try to destroy or tear down everything that God is doing in our lives. No one can throw in my face that I use to pose for men's magazines and I am now writing a book about purity and keeping it holy because I have taken away its power to tear me down by being open about it. Honestly, no one may have even listened to me if that was not my story. It is hard to preach from a place you have never been and it is hard for people to believe that change is possible if they are hearing from a person who has been holy their entire lives.

Therefore, we cannot be ashamed or embarrassed. You can google me and all of the pictures will come up. But guess what, I do not care, I am not ashamed or embarrassed. I am not that person anymore. I walk boldly in my calling, and I profess and proclaim the redemptive work that God has done in my life.

So to you dear sister, do not be embarrassed or ashamed. Do not let fear and regret stifle your calling. Use the things in your past as a testimony. Walk with your head held high. Put on your crown and always remember that you are a daughter of the King.

Self Reflection

What should we do when we take a misstep?

What does no condemnation mean to you in regard to things you've done in your life that you are not proud of?

Answer honestly, how much do the opinions of others affect you?

Are there choices that you made in your past that are keeping you bound by regret? Are you condemning yourself?

List a few scriptures to have with you in weak moments.

Who are three people you can count on to be your accountability? Name them. Reach out to them.

Conclusion & Prayer…

I hope that this will open up a new dialogue for you to have with Christ, yourself and with others. God wants His very best for you. Don't just finish reading and then tuck this book away. Please take some time to ponder the things we have discussed in these four sections. Go back to the parts you need to go over again. Pray about them. Ask God for revelation. Seek His face. Ask Him to show you the areas in your life that are displeasing to Him. Do your very best to live according to His word. And when you stumble, stay down on your knees, repent, pray, get up, and move forward.

Heavenly Father, I thank you for every woman and girl reading this book. I pray that it refreshes their spirit and replenishes their soul. We humbly ask that you speak to our hearts and minds, and help us to see the areas where we are not submitted to You. Forgive us of our sins and help us to walk boldly in our callings with no condemnation. Thank you Lord for Your unending grace and mercy. You love us when we do not even love ourselves. Help us to see beauty in the creation that we sometimes take for granted. We recognize that we are Your daughters, Your princesses, we are heirs to Your throne and we have to conduct ourselves as such.

In Jesus' Name We Pray, Amen.

A Few Facts About Ivonnah

Awesomemazing woman of God. A mother, a former video model, a Sunday school teacher, a mentor, a dancer – who knows how to act, a forever student, my mother only child & second oldest of my dad, I'm a missionary, like Chanel bags, Gucci dresses & YSL shoes, just call me the Phyllis Nefler of the mission field, I like to dress up & look pretty & when I do, I do the most, I have big hair, I love all things girly, I'm cranky in the morning, love 80's music, (my son came out the womb doing the moonwalk), I'm head unicorn tamer and queen sprinkle thrower, I like purple hearts and romantic stuff, I made a vow to the Lord to remain abstinent in 2008, not because it was the cool thing to do, but because God told me to, I'm smart, I want to get married soon, I'm dope, I'm an extreme PTA mom (as my son use to call me) and I'm everyone's favorite Wild N' Out girl, the one with the short hair Better Known As Ivonnah…

I really hope you enjoyed my first book. Please check out Ivonnah.com for more merchandise and updates on All Things Ivy.

www.ingramcontent.com/pod-product-compliance
Lightning Source LLC
LaVergne TN
LVHW041545070426
835507LV00011B/938